APR 1 6 2008

Λ Rainbow Book

DATE DUE

D1302101

Teen GRIEF Relief

Parenting with Understanding,
Support and Guidance

Dr. Heidi Horsley
and
Dr. Gloria Horsley

Rainbow Books, Inc.
F L O R I D A

Library of Congress Cataloging-in-Publication Data

Horsley, Heidi.
 Teen grief relief : parenting with understanding, support, and guidance / Heidi Horsley and Gloria Horsley.
  p. cm.
 ISBN-13: 978-1-56825-110-3 (trade softcover : alk. paper)
 ISBN-10: 1-56825-110-6 (trade softcover : alk. paper)
 1. Teenagers and death. 2. Grief in adolescence. 3. Bereavement in adolescence. I. Horsley, Gloria Call. II. Title.
  BF724.3.G73H67 2007
  155.9'370835—dc22

                          2007018584

Teen Grief Relief:
Parenting with Understanding, Support and Guidance

ISBN-10: 1-56825-110-6 • ISBN-13: 978-1-56825-110-3

Published by Rainbow Books, Inc.

Editorial Offices
P. O. Box 430 • Highland City, FL 33846-0430
(863) 648-4420 • Fax: (863) 647-5951
RBIbooks@aol.com • www.RainbowBooksInc.com

Individuals' Orders
(800) 431-1579 • www.Amazon.com • www.AllBookStores.com • www.BookCH.com

The paper used in this publication meets the minimum requirements of the American National Standard for Information Sciences—Permanence of Paper for Printed Library Materials, ANSI Z39.48-1984.

13 12 11 10 09 08 07   5 4 3 2 1

First Edition. Printed in the United States of America.

To

Scott Preston Horsley II,
Gloria's son and Heidi's brother,
whose death has taught our family
profound love, gratitude, compassion and forgiveness.

&

The Compassionate Friends

Teen GRIEF Relief

Contents

10   Forever in Your Mind   67

11   Now What?   76

Resources: Help and Information for Grieving Teens   79

    Hot Lines   79

    Chat Rooms   79

    Internet Radio   80

    Organizations and Websites   80

References   84

About the Authors

    Heidi Horsley, Psy.D.   86

    Gloria Horsley, Ph.D.   86

Acknowledgments

We acknowledge our husbands Phil and Markus who have been by our sides and shared with us the greatest sorrows, gifts and blessings the world has to offer.

We thank our family members, including the "next generation," for teaching us about love and bringing joy to our lives.

A very big thank you to all of the teens in this book and the teens at The Compassionate Friends National Conferences who shared stories, hopes, dreams and advice. Your insights and your willingness to share are greatly appreciated.

None of this would have happened without the support and encouragement of Pat Loder, Wayne Loder, Dave Pellegrin and all of the angels of The Compassionate Friends who have encouraged our family to share our lives.

Thank you to Toni Robino and Doug Wagner of With Flying Colours Literary Services, and to Betty Wright and Rainbow Books, for top of the line editing and ongoing support and encouragement.

Thank you to Annette McConnell who takes care of Alexander and Samantha and loves them as much as we do. You are so much more than our babysitter; you are part of our family.

A special thank you goes to Eliza Bara who reviewed our manuscript and helped us to bring it up to teenager language and standards.

Lastly, thanks to Maureen Parton who has faithfully kept track of expenses and encouraged us on.

A Note from Dr. Heidi Horsley

When I was 20, I was awakened in the middle of the night with the news that my 17-year-old brother and a cousin had been killed in a car accident. In an instant, my life turned upside down. I couldn't believe it was happening. My brother was a big part of my life, and suddenly he was gone. I was never going to talk to him, see him smile or hear him laugh again. I desperately hoped it was all a bad dream. It wasn't.

People told me I needed to be strong for my parents. I didn't want to cause them any more pain, so I didn't let them see me cry. I hid my grief. Everyone thought I was fine, but I wasn't fine. I was sad, angry and lost. I felt incredibly guilty that my two sisters and I were still alive while our only brother was dead. I felt as if nobody understood what I was going through or how much pain I was in. Those were dark days.

No one could have told me that the pain lessens over time. I wouldn't have believed it. Nobody could have told me anything at that point in my life. I felt so alone. Surprisingly, though, as the months and years passed, I did start to feel better. I've never gotten over Scott's death or stopped wishing he were still alive, but I have learned to live without him, as I know he would have wanted me to do. And even though he's not here with me, he's still my brother, and he'll always hold a place in my heart.

There is hope. You will laugh again, love again and find happiness in your life again.

A Note from Dr. Gloria Horsley

Twenty-four years ago, we lived in upstate New York — Mom, Dad and four kids. Heidi and Rebecca were in college. Heather was 14 and her big brother, Scott, 17, was a junior in high school. Scott, as the girls would tell you, was the brother every girl wanted. He was the catcher on the baseball team and the quarterback on the football team. He had wavy blond hair, big green eyes and a laugh that rocked the world. He loved his family and was especially proud to have three cool sisters.

One rainy night Scott was riding home from a movie with his cousin Matthew when Matthew lost control of the car and hit a cement wall. As two men jumped out of their car to help, Matthew's car caught fire and the gas tank blew up. The boys died together. I was devastated. The pain was almost unbearable at times. My world was shattered. But over time our family got through it.

The teens interviewed for this book want you to know that you can make it through too. No matter how discouraged or hopeless you may feel, please remember that you need not walk alone.

Foreword

I'm very sorry you've experienced a loss. Depending on what's happened, you might be feeling sad, angry, confused, frustrated or helpless. Sixteen years ago, when my brother Rick died and my two children, Stephanie and Stephen, died a few months later, I felt all these emotions and many others. There were days when the pain was so great I didn't know what I was feeling. Other days I was so overwhelmed that I just felt numb — and sometimes that was a blessing.

If you've lost a loved one, you may be worried that you'll start to forget them. You won't. In fact, keeping your loved one alive in your mind and heart is an important part of your healing journey.

Everyone experiences loss differently, and everyone grieves in his or her own way. Therefore, I won't claim to know how you're feeling. What I *will* do is assure you that there's light at the end of the tunnel. You can get through this — and you don't have to do it alone. Connect with people who care about you and want to support you.

The messages from other teens and the insights in this book from Dr. Gloria Horsley and her daughter Dr. Heidi Horsley will give you a starting point on your path to healing the grief of your loss, whatever it may be.

I wish you gentle peace and strong courage.

Pat Loder
Executive Director
The Compassionate Friends

Introduction

To the Parent of a Grieving Teen

We ask a friend to describe a typical teenager. She, being a mother of two teens, takes on the task. Her laundry list includes — considerate, belligerent, defiant, thoughtful, stubborn, resistant, funny, lazy, non-cooperative, lovable and adorable. What a ball of contradiction!

As therapists, we give workshops for parents on helping teenagers deal with grief. We always have a good turnout at these workshops. Parents — just like you who more than likely purchased this book — are eager for our help. They want to know what's normal and what to watch for.

Parents constantly tell us that their teens aren't communicating with them; they specifically want to know how to get their teens to open up more. We also give workshops for grieving teenagers, and they tell us what they need from their parents.

Teens tell us they would open up more, but their parents won't listen and are too busy judging and criticizing them. They also tell us that their parents are controlling, punitive, outdated and out of touch. But on the other hand, they are yearning for parents who will enlighten them and metaphorically "hold their hand."

Parents who come to our workshops are longing for information on how to help their teenagers deal with loss. They worry, and they obsess. They also ask if we have something their teenager could read that might help them with their grief.

In response to parents and teens, we decided to write a book for teens, based on our parent and teen workshops. We even had a title for the book: *Making the Best of the Worst: A Message of Hope for Surviving Teenagers*. We were then advised by our wise publisher that teenagers don't read — once they get the keys to the car. No teenager was going to buy our book. What then?

We knew from doing workshops with parents and from personal experience that parents want help, they want closer, more open relationships with their teens. Teenagers are hurting and angry and want to be understood. Grieving teenagers tell us that hurt, frustration and feeling misunderstood cause them to strike out at those around them. Parents end up resenting the fact that they have to put up with some ugly behavior. Parents talk about the frustration they have at their teen staying out late, getting drunk, having screaming fits, sexual promiscuity, acting defiant and hanging around other angry teenagers. Meanwhile, grieving teenagers have told us that they want to be acknowledged, validated and understood. Now the question became: How do we reach those who need this book most?

We are depending on parents like you to deliver our message for us. We believe that through love, patience, understanding, open communication and just plain timing you will be able to use this book to support your grieving teen. You may even get them to read a few pages. Don't push. Just leave the book around the house, perhaps with a few pages turned back, waiting to be read. Meanwhile, it can give you comfort in knowing that responses like "I don't want to talk about it" are normal. You will receive ideas and suggestions on how to support, comfort and nurture surviving children through the hell of losing a loved one. When you feel empty and out of ideas, pick up this book and leaf through it for advice and positive suggestions. Here is a framework for dealing with teens, while adding some rationale to the crazy world for your teenage griever. We hope that you will also do the exercises included in this book. We believe you will personally benefit from them as well as being an example to your teen.

Teenagers Desire a Democracy — Not a Dictatorship

After years of working with families, we know the best ways to reach teenagers is through a parent. Parents must walk a fine line. While teens want support and empathy with regard to their loss, they do not want to be smothered and micromanaged. The job of a teenager has always been to rebel, develop their own unique personality, and begin to individuate from the family, while the parents' job is to instill values and set limits for the teenager to move against. The idea has always been for the parents to hold tight with an open hand and give wise information, listen and be open to compromise when needed.

While we as parents do not always have to agree with our teens, it is important for parents to say that although they appreciate their teen being so open and honest, they do not agree or approve of what they are hearing. If you have introduced this book into your teen's life, you can just blame it all on us.

Information contained in this book can give you and your teenager direction, comfort and even a sense of humor when dealing with your unbearable loss. It can give you patience in knowing that responses such as the following are normal:

"Life sucks."

"You don't really care about me!"

"I hate living here!"

"I wish I was the one who died."

"My life wasn't supposed to turn out this way."

Don't assume it is personal. It isn't. This is a teen trying to come to terms with a world he or she never anticipated. So — pick up this book, read a few pages, try some of the exercises and encourage your teen to read a few pages. Perhaps you may be able to sit down together at some point and share a few pages together. Help us deliver the message.

Why Teenagers Suffer More

The unfairness of losing a loved one is a devastating shock to teenagers. Teenagers feel immortal; deaths of siblings, parents or friends rock a world that is already in turmoil. Just being a teenager is a painful and uncertain time of life. Hormones are raging and expectations are high. Bereaved adults can take time off from work or go in late, college age kids can drop out for a semester; but, your teenager has to go back to school and keep up a frantic life pace. There is little down time to explore the meaning of their loss. All teenagers have their ups and downs, but what we most want is to give you an idea of how to connect with your bereaved teenager and help them to better cope with their pain and suffering.

What Happens to Friendships

As a parent, you know friendships are pivotal relationships for your teenager. Friends help set the trends and let teenagers know what is cool and what is not. Teenagers tell us that, after a few weeks, many of their old and trusted friends drop by the way side. Listen to Ashley:

"After about a month, I stopped getting invited to hang out with friends. Sure, I could call them, and they would invite me to go along, but I wasn't being asked to go to the movies or party with them. I was so angry that I finally stopped carrying my cell phone."

Ashley's comment is typical of some of the suffering teenagers go through. Bereaved teenagers tell us that they finally gave up on many of their old friends. They tell us that people expected them to get back to "normal." The expectations were too heavy, and they often turned to new relationships. They talk about some new and positive friendships being formed, but on the whole they feel that many of their past friends turned out not to be "true friends" — another loss.

As new friends come along, your teen may gravitate toward angry teens who are dealing with losses of their own. These unhappy, belligerent teens understand what anger is all about and can handle their bereaved friend's mood swings. These are rocky shores, and teens need special support at this time.

Big Three Emotions

There are basically three emotions that may keep your grieving teenager in a state of suffering. The big three are: Anger, Guilt and Shame.

Anger

Anger at losing a loved one is huge for a teenager. By dying, this person has really screwed up their life. Anger can stem from many places. Teens might be angry at the person for abandoning them, angry at God for allowing this to happen, angry at the world for not understanding how difficult it is for the teen. In addition, parents often become overly protective following a death. Teenagers tell us that it is as if their parents have a magnifying glass on them at all times. Teens feel like their parents want them to account for every second in the day. Teens claim that parents are reluctant to turn the car keys over to the teenager, and they want almost constant check ins from the cell phone.

One teenager told us, "It's like I'm under house arrest. Why should I suffer? I didn't wreck the car. I have a valid driver's license. I took Drivers Ed." Teenagers feel cheated and angry when they are treated differently than they were before the death. Their developmental task of becoming more independent has been interrupted.

Guilt

Although your teenager may not really be able to translate feelings into words, the second cause for teenage suffering is guilt. Many teens have guilt and regret that they didn't spend more time with the deceased, or remorse that they didn't treat them better. Here is one example of teen guilt from our Internet radio show, "Healing The Grieving Heart."

Darrell Scott, whose daughter Rachel was murdered in the Columbine High School massacre, discussed on our show the fact that Rachel's brother Craig was very withdrawn for about six months following Rachel's death. Darrell said that he was sure there was something Craig hadn't told him. When Darrell sat down and talked to Craig, his son told him that he had had a fight with Rachel the morning of her death and they had left for school on bad terms. Craig felt that it should have been him. Darrell said that after the talk Craig started to show some marked improvement.

Craig's dad helped Craig to see that their argument was one of a normal response between siblings and that it did not change their love for one another. "It should have been me" or "I should have treated my sibling better" or "I should have prevented the death" are common responses that cause teenagers to suffer.

Shame

A third cause of teenage suffering is shame. Often when teens experience a death they feel all alone. As a parent, I'm sure you are aware, teenagers hate to be different. They long to fit in, be looked up to, be popular, but they don't want to be different or pointed out as the one whose brother, sister or parent died. Your teenager longs to be popular and envied, not pitied. This can be especially difficult if it was a suicide, homicide or if the family member was driving a car in which others were killed.

Sex, Drugs and Alcohol

Angry-, Guilty- and Shame-based bereaved teenagers often have a "live for the moment" attitude and may take more risks than they have in the past. Sex, drugs, and alcohol may appear in a bereaved teen's life. Easing the pain, self-medicating and finding intimacy are common responses to their traumatic loss. An additional concern you might have is the teen who isolates from friends and outside activities. Suffering in silence is never a positive response for your teenager. This is the time to seek guidance for your teen from a therapist who is experienced in treating bereaved teens.

The following are important points that we'd like to review with you regarding grieving teens' behaviors.

ASPECTS OF TEEN GRIEF

1. Developmentally, teenagers understand that death is permanent. Teens tend to stick with intense bereavement emotions for shorter amounts of time than adults. They need to take breaks from their grief so that they will not become too overwhelmed.

2. The developmental task of separation from the family and becoming more autonomous is interrupted by loss. The teenager may become defiant or regress. Parents often become overprotective and more fearful that their child or children will also die.

3. Teenagers don't want to grieve in front of a parent for several reasons. One, they don't want to upset their parent and cause them further pain; two, they don't want to have their parent see them as childish and dependent; and, three, they don't want their parent to get into a competition over whose grief is worse. In other words, a teen as well as a parent may need to be reminded there is no hierarchy of grief.

4. Adolescence is a difficult time to experience a loss. This makes teenagers feel different; they have experienced a non-normative event that many of their friends can't relate to.

No Hierarchy of Grief

"Every loss is unique. The truth is, the worst loss is the one that is happening to you, the one that has picked you up and thrown you down and left you struggling to put your life back together."

— Elizabeth DeVita-Raeburn, author of
*The Empty Room: Surviving the Loss
of a Brother or Sister at Any Age*

How You Can Help Your Teenager

1. By purchasing this book you have already set the tone. Showing your teenager this book and discussing teen loss gives them permission to grieve. You are showing them that you acknowledge and validate their loss. A good thing to say in sibling loss is, "I am here for you, but I do not know how you feel." Or you may even say, "I have lost a child, but I have never lost a sibling. It must be difficult." Or you can acknowledge any loss by saying, "I have never lost a friend. Tell me about it." Another example is a woman who had lost her father at age 8 and her daughter at age 45 to breast cancer. She told her granddaughter, "I know what it is to lose a father, but I've never lost a mother. Could you tell me about it?"

2. Just a reminder that teens need their loss acknowledged and validated, while at the same time they need reassurance that the intensity of their grief won't last forever. This is a fine line to walk because while your teen does not want their pain or grief minimized, they do want to know that they won't always feel this bad. As we have said earlier, teenagers really suffer over loss of friends, while loss of family simply undermines their world.

3. If you can get them to go to teen bereavement groups, this can be very effective. These groups validate and normalize a teen's grief responses, and teens don't feel so alone. Closed chat rooms online can be helpful also but must be monitored carefully.

4. You will be ahead of the game if you will allow teens to finish what they're saying while listening in a non-judgmental way. When listening, try to honor your adolescent's need for the avoidance of intense emotions, while at the same time creating a safe space for your kids to open up and grieve if they need to. Not an easy task, while you may be grieving yourself.

5. Encourage your teenager in creative outlets. There are many examples in this book, including art, music, writing, physical activities and hobbies. If your teen isn't interested, do them yourself. Lead by example. We have personally tried the majority of ideas in this book and found them helpful. Here's an example of how we, as therapists, use these activities in group sessions:

This group of teens had lost a close friend to a car accident — and we used what we call "A Graffiti Wall." We began by unrolling a large, long strip of paper that covered a wall. The teens were than asked to draw and/or write their thoughts and feelings about the death of their friend. "Try to be open and candid," we said. Then, we reminded them that they were in a safe place for inner expression. Colored markers were passed around, and slowly but surely each of them began to write and draw their honest feelings. In the end, it became a powerful and helpful step toward recovery.

How to Approach Your Teen

We suggest you do it like your mother used to get you to take medicine — carefully, thoughtfully and in small doses.

You might begin by saying, "Just try glancing through this book. Even if you don't like it, it might make you feel better."

If that doesn't work, try, "What have you got to lose?"

Once you get the conversation going, even if it is in bits and pieces, you will find an opening. Trust your heart; the ideas will flow.

Don't forget to use this book yourself and make it readily available by leaving it tossed on a sofa, a coffee table, in front of the television — anywhere your teen might easily pick it up and glance through it. You never know when your teenager might read a few pages and surprise you. Listen to what a mother has to say:

I only wish this book had been around twenty years ago when we had a death in our family and my fourteen-year-old said, "Mom, you know the only people who really care about me are the Dead Heads." She was referring to Jerry Garcia and those who followed his band, "The Grateful Dead." I would have suggested to her that she make a CD of her favorite songs and share them with me. At the time I was dumb struck, and my heart felt broken.

When to Seek Professional Help

We wanted to include this in our book because, as we know from personal and professional experience, grief can be as scary for you as a parent — life can feel so out of control. Some of the warning signs that your teenager may need professional help can be confusing, but they are also part of the normal grieving process. As a result, they can be misdiagnosed, turning normal grief into pathology. However, if your child is showing a number of the following behaviors, you need to seek professional help immediately:

1. Suicidal ideations, while feeling hopeless, helpless, worthless
   a. Having a plan; and having the means to carry out the plan
2. Sleep problems
3. Giving away possessions
4. Isolation
5. Disregard for personal hygiene
6. Drugs/alcohol use
7. Grades that are dropping ever lower
8. Recent change in friendships
9. Ditching school
10. Unsuccessful in all areas of life — not involved in any activities, clubs, hobbies, after school programs, sports or job

One of the questions we ask bereaved teens to help them differentiate grief from depression: How would you feel if the deceased person walked into the room at this very moment?

If your teen answers that their sadness would lift and they would feel just great, they are most likely suffering normal bereavement.

But if too much is going wrong in your teen's life and you still feel uneasy, again, our suggestion is that you get professional help.

We truly hope this book will be used by your teen to find ideas, comfort and grief relief and to know that other teens have been there before them and made it, and they need not walk alone.

PART I

Facing
the
Worst-Case
Scenario

1

Living In an Upside-Down World

"It's like you're in a foreign country now,
and you were just dropped there, and now you have
to learn to make yourself adapt to this new world
and this new way of life, and it's not easy."

Lauren and Kerri Kiefer, radio show guests on
"Healing the Grieving Heart"

Show Topic: The World Lost a Hero, We Lost Our Brother

Lauren & Kerri's older brother, Firefighter Michael Vernon Kiefer,
was murdered in the September 11th World Trade Center attacks.

If you're reading this, you've probably had someone die who was very important to you. You may feel angry, sad, empty, confused, exhausted, anxious, helpless or all those things at once. Or the pain may be so overwhelming that you don't know what you're feeling.

And chances are you're thinking:

Nobody understands what I'm going through.

And questioning:

Why did this have to happen?

It may seem that you've lost your way — or even yourself.

Unfortunately, thousands of other teens are facing terrible losses right now too; and thousands more have already been down a similar path. Everyone's loss is different. No one knows exactly what anyone else is feeling. Sometimes, though, hearing about what other people have gone through and how they handled it may help.

All through this book you'll hear from other teens who wanted to share some of their thoughts and insights. Even though they don't know you, they can relate to tough times.

We all want to give you hope and assure you that there's light at the end of this tunnel. We want you to hang in there. Things really will get better, even though that might be impossible to believe right now. We also want to share some ideas on how you can get some relief and make a connection — not by sugarcoating reality or avoiding it, but by taking care of yourself and taking small steps that will make the road a little less bumpy and the hills a little less steep.

You're Not Crazy:
The Mind-Body Connection

Crazy as it sounds, feeling like you're going crazy is one of the most normal ways to feel after you experience the death of someone close to you. The feelings of craziness come from experiencing so many thoughts and emotions at once. It's sort of like your brain is playing six or seven radio stations with different kinds of music all at once. It's a racket that can't be subdued. It just keeps on playing and playing, until you think you can't take it another minute.

You're experiencing the normal biology of grief, sorrow and sadness, if you're:

- Walking around in a daze feeling lost, alone or empty;

- So pissed off that you want to hit someone or something;

- Sure that no one understands how you feel;

- Hurting too much to think;
- Feeling crazy with grief;
- Out of control; or
- Too shocked and too numb to feel anything at all.

We want you to know that your brain and your body are doing exactly what they're supposed to do after you suffer the death of someone close to you. You don't have control over these physiological effects, but there are things you can do to make yourself feel a little better or at least a little more calm for a few minutes at a time. Knowing that what you're feeling is normal may not make things any better, but it can give you some reassurance and comfort.

Teen Loss Vignettes

We have collected some brief vignettes from other bereaved teens that you might relate to. Don't feel you have to read them all. Pick the ones that relate to your situation.

"I'm really angry at my sister. She jumped off a bridge and killed herself. I don't get it. I went through her room and found her dentist and orthodontist appointments and saw a bunch of things marked on her calendar for the whole rest of the year. Why did she make these plans — if she knew she was going to kill herself?"

— *Mikiko, 14*

"I keep asking myself where my big brother is. It's weird — I'm the oldest now. My brother always took all the heat for me. He had to make sure that we got in on time and that the garbage was out and the lawn got mowed. I don't think my mom and dad realized how little I really did. But now all that stuff is up to me. My little sister doesn't do anything but walk the dog. I really hate being the oldest; it sucks. It isn't working for me at all. I'm a soccer player, not a garbage man.

Besides, my brother is dead, dead, dead. It's like everything is going wrong — and I can't stop it.

— Malcolm, 14

"Dad was my basketball coach and a great friend. He was the kind of Dad who would cook and tuck us into bed at night. He had us every other weekend and two weeks during the summer. They said he dropped dead of a heart attack in the parking lot of an airport. Nobody saw him until it was too late. Man, I really miss him.

— Lance, 17

"Annette and I had a major fight the day she was killed. We shared the same room, and she was a mess. Left all her clothes on the floor. I'd complain to Mom, but she wouldn't do anything. She said she didn't get along with her sister when they were kids, and now they're close. I said, 'Fine, but that doesn't help me now.' I finally took a piece of tape and put it on the floor to divide the room and told Annette not to cross the tape with any of her junk. Well, I came home from school, and she was wearing my belt. I was furious. She took it off and threw it at me and said, 'You're the meanest sister I know.' Then her friend's mom picked her up to go ice skating, and that was the last time I saw her. The police said the car was hit by a drunk driver. It's not fair. Lots of sisters don't get along, but this doesn't happen to them."

— Stephanie, 16

"I now have two brothers and no sister. I really hate the fact that Veronica got a brain tumor. She was so cute, and I loved having a little sister. Being the oldest, she was like a living doll for me. When she was born, Mom let me feed her and let my friends hold her. I even let her come on dates with me sometimes. My boyfriend thought it was a little weird, but I loved it. When she started to cry that her head hurt, I'd have her sit on my lap and read her a story. I miss her so much. I can't wait to get married and have a little girl. I'll definitely name her Veronica."

— Miranda, 17

"My mom was diagnosed with pancreatic cancer before Christmas. I felt sorry for her when all her hair fell out. We gave her a funny hat for Christmas. She loved it. Six months later she died. I miss her so much.
— *Brenda, 13*

2

Emotional Extremes

"I remember being a teenager and just being fearless
and careless about everything. Not really having
any particular desire to protect myself or be safe, and
I don't know if I felt like I was invulnerable or if I just
didn't care. I think part of it was that the loss is
intense enough that you kind of wish it had been
you and not your brother."

Ben Sieff, radio show guest on "Healing the Grieving Heart"

Show Topic: When a Sibling Is Murdered

Ben's brother Tim was murdered.
Ben serves on the National Board of
The Compassionate Friends.

Teens often say that since they've had someone close to them die,
they seem to be set off by the smallest things. It scares them that they get
so sad, angry and upset.

John tells us that in his heart he knows it's not okay to strike out at
his brother, but since his dad died, "My whole body is on edge."

John is undergoing a normal response to a stressful event known as the fight-or-flight response. It's the physical response that gave our prehistoric ancestors the surge of energy they needed to face danger or flee from it. When you hear, smell or see something that triggers thoughts of your loss, hormones speed through your body and brain, serving as chemical messengers that warn of danger. Basically, they're alerting you to fight or run.

Although this response is helpful when your life is being threatened or you need to respond quickly in an actual crisis, it can wreak havoc when it's triggered again and again. For one thing, it's exhausting. Like with John and the cavemen, the hormone surge makes us feel jumpy and anxious, and when levels start to drop again, we feel exhausted. Unfortunately, once the hormones are released into our systems, we have to ride it out, but there are things we can do to make the ride a little smoother.

See if you relate to Patrick's story about how fight-or-flight caught him off guard, then check out the remedies for how to deal with it.

"I was getting my books out of my locker when a guy I used to be friends with but hardly ever see anymore put his hand on my shoulder and said he'd heard my dad died and asked how I was doing. It really freaked me out. My chest tightened, and I felt like I was being crushed. My body tensed, and I felt my eyes go wide. I wanted to run, jam my fist into my locker or get the hell out of there. Then I thought I was going to cry. I kept thinking: Get hold of yourself. I wanted to just drop on the floor. I just couldn't get a grip. I finally said, 'I can't talk about it now.' He understood and walked off. I just needed to be alone. I missed my next class. It took me a whole hour to get a hold of myself."

— *Patrick, 16*

Patrick's mind goes into overdrive, his body takes a hormonal hit, his pupils dilate and his blood vessels constrict. His heart pumps faster. His oxygen levels increase. Patrick — like his primitive ancestor — is ready to run or lash out. But he's standing in a hallway at school, so neither is a good option. Instead he fights back the tears welling up in his eyes and swallows the lump in his throat and tries to act like everything's cool while his body and mind are going wild.

How to Deal with Overdrive

Since the fight-or-flight response (what we're calling *overdrive* here) always comes by surprise, it's helpful if you have a few options ready ahead of time. Read the list below and make notes on the ones you plan to try.

- Recognize what's going on: "My mind has triggered a hormonal hit. My body is responding in a normal way. I can hold on. I am safe, and this will pass."

- Breathe deeply. Oxygen helps to disperse the hormones.

- Yawn. This will relax your throat when you have a lump that won't go away.

- Get a drink of water.

- Go to the bathroom, wash your hands and put a cold towel on the back of your neck.

- Look out a window.

- Go to your guidance counselor's office at your school. You can talk to the counselor or just sit; take a break from questions your teachers and fellow students may have. Eat a snack. Hormonal responses decrease your blood sugar.

- Move your body. Dance, run, swim, play tennis, walk — whatever. Getting some exercise will help your body relax and your mind clear.

- Listen to music alone in your room.

- Meditate.

With all that said, sometimes crying, shouting, screaming or hitting a pillow helps. There's nothing wrong with crying. In fact, it actually helps us relax. Research has found that crying lowers blood pressure, pulse rate and body temperature and results in more synchronized brain-wave patterns. In other words, it reduces tension. It's a natural healing mechanism, so, by all means, put it to use.

Why Did This Happen?

One of the hardest things about loss is that we rarely get an answer to the question: "Why did this happen?" And if we do get an answer, it's rarely the answer we want. So, a part of our brain keeps asking that question, because it hasn't got an answer that it can completely accept and "compute." The problem is that even if you end up with a reason you can accept, it won't bring back the person you've lost.

So, just for the time it takes you to read this book, we're going to ask you to try something:

When the question "why" enters your mind, say "pass" (silently or out loud) and allow yourself to skip that question for now.

3

What If You Don't Want to Talk About It?

"You cannot mourn unless you claim your story.
Telling the story is a huge step in the healing process,
much more important than any of us realized."

*Elizabeth DeVita-Raeburn, radio show guest on
"Healing the Grieving Heart"*

Show Topic: Death of a Sibling

*Elizabeth's brother Ted died from a rare autoimmune disease.
Her story was loosely portrayed in the John Travolta
made-for-TV movie,* The Boy in the Plastic Bubble.
Elizabeth is the author of
The Empty Room: Surviving the Loss
of a Brother or Sister at Any Age.

"Sometimes I'd think I saw a light at the end of the tunnel, but then at other times I'd think the light was really the light on the front of a train heading toward me. Either way, I didn't want to talk about it."

— Carl, 17

"My dad tries to talk to me, but I just pull away. I'm really not sure why. I just don't want to open myself up to a lot of stuff. It seems like the more I give him, the more he wants. I can't just say something and let it go at that. I don't want to be in pain and I don't want him to be in pain. I'm just trying to be a 'good kid.' I just want to be a normal family again."

— *Stacey, 16*

"I'm still pissed at my dead brother. He was doing drugs every weekend and was out all night. It freaked my mother out nonstop. When I turned 16, they didn't want me to drive at night all because my brother was out of control. I really just don't like talking about him."

— *Lance, 18*

Everyone responds differently to traumatic events, and the way you feel can change from day to day, even from moment to moment. Sometimes you need to be alone, and sometimes you need to let other people in. Ironically, the times you need to let people in are often the times when you want to be alone.

It's perfectly okay not to want to talk about your loss, but it's not okay never to talk about it. If you feel like you can't talk to your parents, consider talking with other people, especially those who have experienced losses of their own. At the very least, make a visit to an online chat room that is specifically for teens dealing with loss and death. Check out . . .

The Compassionate Friends
www.CompassionateFriends.org

You can also write in the online journal, Legacy.com, where you can anonymously connect with other teens who understand how things are for you. There might be someone online who has something difficult to say that you need to hear, or you might say just the right thing to help someone else.

Understanding and Coping With Your Parents

After the death of a family member, dealing with your parents can be one of the hardest parts of getting through the day. Chances are that your parents don't know what you're really thinking and feeling, and you don't know what they're really thinking and feeling. Bridging this gap can make a big difference in how your family grieves, heals and maintains a connection with the one they've lost.

Parents Who Have Lost One of Their Children Tell Us

"Since his brother Paul died, Ryan wears headphones all the time. The only time I hear a sound from him is when he says a couple of lyrics. He doesn't even sing them, just says them. I feel like it's his way of shutting his dad and me out."

"I'm so concerned about Rachel. She was such a good kid before her brother died. She doesn't obey the rules anymore, and I think she's having sex with her boyfriend. I'm sure she's drinking and using drugs. I just don't know what to do. She hates her father's new wife, and I have to work full time. Our house has become a hangout for a bad crowd. I was an only child, and I hated it. I never wanted this to happen to Rachel."

"All Rick does since his sister was killed is watch TV and play video games in the basement. Sometimes I go down and he's lying with his face to the wall. I think he's crying, but I don't know what to do. Guys don't want to cry in front of their dads, so I just quietly leave the room. I'm hoping that when football season starts, that'll snap him out of it."

"I took Diane to buy clothes yesterday, and I was shocked when I took a blouse into the dressing room for her and saw long scratches and gashes on her arms. When I said, 'What happened?' she covered up her arms and looked very nervous and guilty. When I got back home I cornered her brother and asked him if he knew what was going on, he said, 'Surprised you haven't noticed it before. She's been chewing her nails and cutting her arms since Roger hung himself.' I called the family physician and he said I need to get her to a counselor. Her brother's death has been a trauma for all of us, but I didn't know it went so deep with Diane."

"I am so crazy since Calvin died of a drug overdose. I check Janet and John's room on a regular basis for any sign that they're using. I check their drawers when they leave for school and even stooped so low as to read Janet's journal. I feel so guilty that we didn't stop Calvin. We knew he was partying every weekend, but his grades were good. My husband finally confronted me. He said, 'You have got to have some trust. You're making everyone's life hell.' I know he's right, and I'm trying, but it isn't easy."

How to Help Your Parents Help You

If your parents or other people are trying so hard to get you to open up that you're feeling like you want to crank up the iPod and never talk again, consider sharing this list of tips with them. Young people tell us that sharing these ideas really helped to get them some space. Before you share it, you might want to revise or delete some of these items and write some of your own. Then, you might want to run the list by your parents and get their input.

1. Talk about the loss, but in small doses. I want to know that loss and death aren't taboo subjects.

2. Ask open-ended questions: "How has it been for you since the death of your friend?"

3. You can explain, but don't lecture. I really hate the lectures, especially when I'm trapped in the car with you.

4. Accept that what I may be feeling is normal adolescent anger, survivor guilt or the feeling that life is unfair.

5. Tell us how you're feeling, and leave it at that. You could say, "I miss John so much today." You don't have to say anything else. We get it.

6. If there's something about the loss that you have to talk to me about, set a time limit and keep it to 15 minutes or less. I just can't stay with you for much longer than that.

7. I'm already feeling the pressure of being judged and criticized by other people, including some of my friends. I need your support more than your criticism right now.

8. Remember that I'm a teenager and try not to take the way I respond to you so personally.

9. Give me age appropriate freedom and don't smother or micromanage me.

10. Keep talking to me. Even if I'm not responding, I'm listening.

Express Yourself

Since everyone grieves differently, you're the only one who knows the best way for you to express your feelings. You might want to vent by running, roller-blading, skateboarding, bike riding, surfing, dancing or doing something else that takes a lot of physical energy. Or you might want to let your feelings out by playing a sport or a musical instrument, by writing songs or poetry or by keeping a diary or journal.

It can be helpful to write in a diary, because you can look back and see how your healing is going. You'll have "proof" that your heart is feeling a little lighter as time passes. Or you'll be able to see that you're feeling worse and may need to get more support or help from others.

Although everyone mourns losses differently, there are some things about the grieving process that are similar for everyone. We hope that reading entries from Lauren's diary will increase your understanding and bring you some comfort.

2002 — Lauren's Diary

Death Day — May 3

"When I looked out the window of our house and saw two men dressed in Army uniforms, it felt like being hit by a ton of bricks. I knew something had happened to Billy. I didn't want my mom to open the door. The men's faces said it all. My brother had been shot by a sniper in Iraq."

May 4

"I kept waking up last night, thinking Billy isn't really dead. I feel numb. I keep having these waves of sadness and anger and feel like I could lose my mind. I can't believe how helpless I feel. In my mind, I know he isn't coming back, but then I hear a sound and expect him to walk in the door. I can't help checking my email for a picture or a note from him. I've tried to find all the emails he ever sent me. I couldn't stop crying when I read his last email: 'Be a good kid and don't do anything I wouldn't do. Love, Billy.' But then I just kept thinking he'd email me or walk in the door."

May 5

"It sort of feels like I've been having a tantrum. I always believed that if you wanted something badly enough you could get it. I've kicked, cried and screamed, but it doesn't bring him back. This sounds strange, but what seems to help me most is drinking a lot of water, stretching and taking short walks. I also slept with my dog last night. It felt so good to hug something warm."

May 15

"We buried Billy today at the Arlington Military Cemetery in Washington, DC. It's the one where Kennedy is buried. We had a busload of friends come, and the guy who was head of the cemetery got kind of upset because he thought we were a tour bus that was just sight-seeing without respect for the dead. We wanted to go to the cemetery because we didn't get to see his body. That was hard for me because I really wanted to say goodbye and hug him for the last time. At first, seeing the casket was pretty scary, but I think it was good to see it. Now I know that's where he'll be. His body, I mean. For some reason, my feelings seem to be a little more under control. It's like I've let something go that I needed to let go."

May 22

"Sometimes I feel like I have a hole in my stomach and chest. Sometimes I feel guilty. Why wasn't it me? It's hard to believe this much pain is supposed to be part of life. I just want to feel normal. I keep clinging to my daily routines. I take really long showers and spend a lot of time brushing my hair and getting ready for school. It seems like I'm living in a bad dream, my life is moving in slow motion. I don't like to watch the news or see the headlines in the newspaper. Seems like something bad is always happening. When I wake up in the morning, I really have to push myself to get up and face things. Last weekend I just stayed in bed until noon, but that wasn't any better than facing things. At least at school I have to pay attention to something other than Billy. I just wish I didn't have to walk through the halls between classes. I can't look at anyone without being afraid they're going to say something that will make me cry. It's kinda like I'm a water balloon. The slightest touch from a friend and there'll be water everywhere. After a whole day of that, I'm so exhausted that I fall asleep the minute I get home. And a couple hours later, I have to do the waking-up thing all over."

July 10

"My biggest problem right now is my parents. They're treating me like a baby. I wish they would just trust me. They want to know everywhere I go and everything I'm going to do. Sometimes I don't know where we're going. It's summer — we might decide to go to a movie rather than the beach. I hate crying in front of my parents. It makes me feel like a baby, and I can see that it really hurts them. I sometimes feel like a bug under a magnifying glass. I just wish they would trust me. Losing someone is hard enough as it is without having to deal with parents who are trying to make up for the fact that they couldn't protect Billy in Iraq."

September 5

"It's actually good to be back in school. Never thought I'd prefer school over summer. I see my parents less now, so we're getting along better. We started going as a family to a self-help group called The Compassionate Friends. I like their motto, 'You need not walk alone.' I meet with a group of kids who have had siblings die. We had a big discussion last week about high-risk behaviors and that we should be careful about dulling our pain with drugs or alcohol. I actually feel pretty normal again when I go to the meetings. Finally."

December 25

"This is our first Christmas without my brother. It was a really hard day, and I had to keep reminding myself that if I could just get through this one day, next year will be better. My counselor at school told me about something she calls 'the rule of four.' It goes like this. During the first year, when you do something like playing a game you used to play with your brother, it really hurts. The second year, when you play the game, you think about your brother but it doesn't hurt so much. The third year, you think about your brother, but the pain is even less. The fourth year, you just play ball. So this Christmas really hurt, but then it should get better and better."

2003

January 12

"It's Billy's birthday. My mom put a rose in the front hall and lit a candle by it. I'm not sure why, but that made me feel good. It sounds like something from a ghost story, but I had a really strange feeling that he was there. Not like a ghost story. It's hard to describe. Mom even had a birthday cake for him. After dinner we sang 'Happy Birthday' and we all blew out the candles. I had tears running down my face. My dad turned to me and gave me a big hug. I try to remember 'the rule of four' and tell myself that the first birthday will be the hardest. Maybe next year I'll stop looking for Billy when I see someone on the ski hill with a red jacket."

May 3

"My grieving-teen group warned me that the second year can be really rough, and they were right. The first year, I was kind of proud of myself that I got through it, but none of my friends want to have me call and say, 'Hey, guess what — this is Billy's death date.' Mom put a rose on the table and lit a candle. Dad suggested that we all write Billy a note. We read the notes and then burned them. Dad and I went to the nursery and bought a rosebush. We planted it in our garden and mixed the ashes with the dirt. I got the feeling that Dad also felt like Billy was there, like I did."

December 23

"We're going to my Aunt Marjorie's for Christmas. Mom says that the first year is a stay-at-home year, but the second year we need to get back into the world. I'm looking forward to a change of scene. I'll think of Billy and cry in my pillow. Mom set the rose and candle out while we were packing. She also packed Billy's special ornament. The one he painted in third grade. I'm sure he knows we'll never forget him."

2005

January 12

"I just realized that I haven't picked up my journal for a while. This year I'm really starting to feel better. It's Billy's birthday, and we invited some of his friends from high school over for pizza. They're college guys and are really cute. I can't believe I'm thinking about cute guys and having fun again. I know Billy is looking out for me and wants me to be happy. I can feel him sometimes. I know what he'd tell me in certain situations if he were really here, and it feels good to have conversations with him in my head. Sometimes it's very comforting. The third year has been pretty good, and I think I'll feel even better in the fourth year. The rosebush is getting big, and Mom put one of its red roses on the table with the candle. I know she'll always feel connected to him like I do. I'm volunteering to help run the sibling discussions in my teen-grief group. It hurts me when we get a new member, but it's good to let them know that it happened to me and I'm here for them."

PART II

Surviving

the

Pain

4

One Minute at a Time

"The definition of surviving is actually rising to act,
and I think if you're going to survive the grief, survive the loss of
a loved one, then you have to eventually get up, you gotta get
back up eventually, so don't give up."

*Scott Mastley, radio show guest on
"Healing the Grieving Heart"*

Show Topic: Surviving a Sibling

*Scott's brother Chris was killed in a car accident.
Scott is the author of the book,* Surviving a Sibling.

"So, I know that death's part of life. So what? It doesn't make my
brother's death any easier to take."

— *Miguel, 14*

What we know and what we feel are often at odds with each other,
especially after we experience a trauma. For kids like Miguel, it's even
harder. When you lose someone on top of everything else, it's no wonder

you feel overwhelmed. Although you might feel like withdrawing, connecting with other people by hearing their stories and possibly sharing yours is a good step. It can help your mind catch up with your feelings and heal some of the emotional pain.

We recently got together with a group of teens to discuss their take on grief and loss, and we'd like to share some of their thoughts and ideas with you. The people in the group were Adam, Carmen, Temera, Justin, Michael and Kayla. We sat in the circle with them but let them know that we were there to listen and that we'd add our thoughts after they all had a chance to share theirs. This is how it went.

The group is quiet for a minute before Adam, 18, begins:

"I told my mother that the Dave Matthews Band are the only ones that care about each other." He shakes his head. "I don't know why I said such a stupid thing. My sister was killed in a head-on with a drunk driver, and I miss fighting with her. You might say we had a love/hate relationship. Sometimes I told her I wished she'd drop dead, and now she is. I feel like it should have been me. Sometimes I feel so guilty that I feel like I'm gonna lose my mind . . .The DMB concerts actually make me feel good, though. And my friends are cool. Drugs and sex help, too. I mean, life's short. My sister proved it."

"It doesn't sound like your way of dealing is really working for you," says 17-year-old Carmen. "My dad's dead. He was a hero — he was a firefighter and he died trying to save people — but so what? That doesn't make it any easier for me to go on. I hate being different. The kid with the dead dad. But we all need to try to move on. I think we should try to do something good with . . . what's happened to us. Or else it's like they died for nothing."

Adam looks thoughtful but doesn't say anything.

"My sister died when I was ten," says Temera, who's 13 now. "She was sixteen and, according to my mother, the perfect child. She had beautiful hair and beautiful skin, and she could play the piano like a professional and always kept her things picked up. There's this old song my mother loves to sing. It goes something like, 'Only the good die young..' How can you compete with that?"

"I kinda know how you feel," says Justin, 15. "I had a tough time living in the same house with my sister, too. She was a real pain, and my parents hardly saw any of it. She hogged the bathroom and hid food from me. She called me the little rat and told her friends that I was the one who was a real pain. We fought over everything from games to who got to sit where. I knew she and her friends were smoking pot in the back yard and doing drugs in the woods, but she said that if I told Mom and Dad she'd kill me, and she probably would have but she killed herself instead. I guess I shouldn't say she killed herself. She really overdosed at a rave. At least that's what the police said. I don't know what to do with myself. In lots of ways, my life is harder since she isn't here; my mom is crying all the time and my dad is staying late at work. I'm just trying to keep a low profile."

"I hear ya," says Michael, 14. "I'm trying to keep a low profile, too, and just live a normal life, but my parents are all over me. My mom and dad are divorced, but she still has my dad pick me up at school right after the football games are over so I can't hang out for even a half-hour. They don't trust me at all. Just because my brother was dumb enough to ride with a drunk friend doesn't mean *I'm* going to do the same thing and get killed, but they obviously can't see that."

"It sounds like you guys' brothers and sisters caused some problems for you, and still do, but do you have good memories, too?" asks Kayla, 15. "I mean, do you think about those sometimes? I really miss my brother Mark. He was my guardian angel and my best friend. When my dad left my mom, it was Mark that taught me to play baseball and basketball and ride a skateboard. Mom had to go back to work and Mark would hang out with me every day after school. He always let me hang out with his friends, too, and he'd get mad if they were jerks to me. I asked Mom why God would take my brother, and she said that God only wants the best. Well, she's right — Mark was the best. I don't know — I guess I just hope you guys don't forget the times like that that you had with your brothers and sisters."

We shared with the group the same ideas we're sharing with you.

- When someone you counted on in your life dies, it's normal to feel as if there's a hole in your heart.

- Having problems with a family member or friend is part of finding out who you are.

- Comfort that you don't count on or expect can come from sharing with other people who understand what you're going through.

- There's always someone who wants to hear what you have to say and help you. If you can't reach someone you know, connect with someone through one of the hot lines or chat rooms that we list at the back of the book.

5

There's Nothing Easy About This

"I had a youth pastor that came into my life and he
saw what was happening with all of my anger,
and he said, 'Craig, forgiveness is like setting a prisoner free
and then finding out that prisoner is you.'"

Craig Scott, radio show guest on
"Healing the Grieving Heart"

Show Topic: Grieving the Loss of a Sibling and Friends:
The Columbine Tragedy

Craig witnessed the murder of his sister
Rachel and 10 classmates at Columbine High School.
Craig supported students and families after the Virginia Tech
massacre and has appeared on Dateline,
Oprah *and* Good Morning America,
and speaks nationally about forgiveness and compassion.

The years from 12 to 20, although filled with promise, are likely to
be the most challenging, confusing, frustrating and stressful years of
your life. Your mind and body are rapidly growing and changing, and

you barely have time to get used to one change before another occurs. It's no surprise that most teens have some intense physical, mental and emotional stress. For those reasons, the teen years are the most difficult time to deal with loss and death. Chances are, you were already feeling overwhelmed or stressed out in some ways before the loss occurred, and now everything feels 10 times worse. Loss creates change, and more change isn't something you want or need right now.

To make things worse, the part of your brain that's in charge of controlling your emotions, restraining impulses and making rational decisions (the prefrontal cortex) is going through a huge growth spurt. From about age 12 until about 20, your brain is developing new pathways that are changing the way your mind works, so you can feel strongly about something today but feel very differently about it a few weeks or months from now. Within a few years, you might feel the opposite of how you feel now. Strange but true. On the positive side, when the "rewiring" is finished, your brain will be able to sort, compare and process information in a much more flexible and efficient way than it does now. It's sort of like installing a new operating system in your computer.

Unfortunately, the future of your re-wire doesn't do you any good right now. For the time being, the unpleasant reality is that you have the potential to short-circuit, lash out and make some poor decisions. That doesn't mean you can't ever be in control; it just means that, especially under the stress, you may say or do some things you wish you hadn't.

Three things kids tell us they've done that have made a big difference:

- Taken good care of themselves (eight hours of sleep, regular meals, exercise);

- Stayed close to the people who care about them; and

- Connected with people who have been through something similar.

Teens Tell Us That Loss Is Hard Because

- It makes them feel uncertain. They were already asking, "Where do I belong? How do I fit in?" before their loss, and now these questions seem more difficult, if not impossible, to answer.

- Loss makes you feel different from your friends. It can make you stand out in a way that you don't want to stand out.

- After a loss, your parents may become overprotective or treat you as if they don't trust you, just when you're craving more freedom and independence. On one hand, you also want them to protect and nurture you, but on the other, you resent them for it.

- You feel sad but don't want to cry in front of other people.

- Sometimes you want to forget about the loss, pretend it didn't happen, and just have fun again. And when you want that, you tend to feel guilty.

- You sometimes feel as if you have no control over your emotions.

- You don't know which feelings are "normal" and which ones might mean you need help.

It's Common to Experience

- Survival Guilt — "It should have been me."

- Magical Thinking — "If only I had done things differently, he/she wouldn't have died."

- Regrets — "I wish I wouldn't have had a fight with him before he left." "I never told him how much he meant to me."

Being a "Survivor" Is Difficult Because

- If a family member has died, not only are you suffering from losing them but you're also dealing with losing the way your parents and family life used to be. You have a double loss.

- Parents sometimes focus too much on your life and projects.

- You're often the forgotten mourner, overlooked, unacknowledged or ignored. People tend to say, "It must be really hard for your parents," or "Be strong for your parents."

Thoughts from Teens
Who Have Lost Loved Ones

Here's what other teens said they would like parents, relatives and friends to know.

"Even though I may not look like it, I am grieving!"

"I like to hear about my dad, but my mom can't seem to stop once she gets going. I wish she'd just talk about him for a few minutes at a time."

"It's okay if you want to talk about my mom who died, but don't pressure me to talk about her."

"I love my big brother, but he was human like the rest of us. Now that he's dead, my mom acts like he was some kind of superman."

"I miss my sister more than anything, but I'm not her and I'll never be her. Sometimes I feel like my mom and dad want me to take her place."

"I want my privacy. I hate it when my mom stands outside my bedroom door and tries to hear what I'm doing. If I feel like crying, I want to be alone. I don't want an audience."

"I know it's really hard on my mom and dad that my brother died, but now they act like they don't trust me. They want to know everything I do and who I'm with, and I'm not allowed to ride in the car if one of my friends is driving. I just want to be treated like a normal kid. I know my parents are scared, but they can't expect me to live my life like that."

"Just once I wish my mom would say, 'This must be really hard for you,' or something like that. She's so caught up in her own grief that she doesn't even notice what I'm going through."

"I don't expect my parents to let me do whatever I want, but I think they should give me enough credit that we should be able to meet halfway on some things."

"I can take care of myself, but it's pretty scary to see my dad falling apart all the time. I mean, if something happens to me or my sister, I'm not so sure that he could even help us. I'm not saying he shouldn't cry about my mom dying. I just want to know he's still there for us."

6

Watching for Trouble Signs

"One thing about anger is it's a very strong and powerful emotion, and
sometimes we're more comfortable being stuck
in anger than feeling helpless or even feeling guilty, and
so we stay in anger because it feels powerful."

*Allie (Alicia Sims) Franklin, radio show guest on
"Healing the Grieving Heart."*

Show Topic: Am I Still a Sister?

*Allie's brother Austin died from a rare childhood cancer.
Allie is the author of* Am I Still a Sister? *and co-author
of* Footsteps Through Grief, The Other Side of Finding Grief *and*
Finding Your Way Through Grief. *Allie was a keynote speaker at the
2001 and 2005 World Gathering on Bereavement.*

"The tricky thing about trouble signs is that they're easy to spot in
somebody else's life and hard to see in our own."

— *Pat, 17*

Pat's right, but since everyone grieves differently, it can be hard to tell whether what you're feeling is normal or not. So, before assessing your own situation, read the scenarios below and consider whether you think the people involved might need some help or support.

Brittany tells us that when her sister died of leukemia, she had survivor guilt. "I kept asking myself, 'Why didn't God take me?' I should have been able to protect my little sister. I know it wasn't rational, but that's the way I felt."

Preston's grades dropped. "Man, I couldn't do math or memorize anything. My mind kept wandering, and I just wanted to get out of the room."

Maddie speaks of becoming reclusive. "I just wanted to avoid people. Either they made me feel like I was some poor, unfortunate thing or they wanted me to 'get over it.' I started sneaking beer and wine into my room and drinking by myself. It helps me sleep. It's not that big a deal — I only drink a little."

Gemma tells us she had some mood changes. "I admit that after we moved, I got more moody, and I'd get really mad at my little brother when he got into my stuff. I was totally over the top. I even started stealing things. I mean, from stores. Stuff I didn't even want all that much."

Ahmad hates being singled out, different. "I just wanna be like everybody else, not the kid who walks down the hall and everybody looks at him like 'He's the guy whose dad was killed in an airplane accident.' That's why I don't want to talk about it. I wear my headphones everywhere. It's a lot better than crying."

"I hate breaking down in front of my parents," Angelica confides. "I know it causes them more pain, plus I'm supposed to be growing up and taking more responsibility. Being emotional with them makes me feel like a baby. It's bad enough having them want to know everywhere I go and what time I'll be home. Just because my brother shot himself doesn't mean I will. I feel like I'm living under a microscope."

"The funny thing is, I didn't even know how much I loved my

grandma until she died," Will says. "During the wake, I went in her basement and played strip poker with my cousins and kids I didn't even know and drank beer. I didn't want to see my dad cry. Since then I've been drinking a lot more on weekends. It's a good way to relax."

"It's so weird, I keep looking for my sister," Rick says. "I know she's dead, but when I see a girl with blond hair I think it's her. It's ridiculous, but the first year she was gone, I'd be walking around looking for her and not even know that's what I was doing for, like, an hour. I also had these waves of grief, and I didn't know when they'd hit me. Sometimes I just had to leave the room and go cry in the bathroom. But you can't leave class all the time, and I just had to hold it in a lot of the time."

What's Normal and What's Not

Brittany has "survivor guilt," and while it's painful, it's normal. If we think we could have stopped something bad from happening or we could have controlled to whom it happened, we believe we have control over life. The fact is, there was nothing Brittany could have done about her sister's death. Some things are out of our control. Your father can be standing in line at a convenience store when someone walks in and pulls out a gun. You can be on the beach and a giant wave caused by an earthquake washes your friend away.

Preston's inability to concentrate is also normal during the first year after a loss. Kids often report a temporary drop in grades. Grieving takes a lot of energy, making it even more important for you to eat healthy food, drink lots of water and get some exercise every day.

Maddie may have a problem. Isolating herself and drinking is clearly becoming a habit. It's also a high-risk behavior, and it sounds as if Maddie doesn't think it's a problem.

Another person displaying high-risk behavior is Gemma. Even though it's not unusual for kids who are grieving to try to fill the empty pit with material possessions, shoplifting can get Gemma into serious trouble and make her life that much more difficult. She might even be at risk of spending time in juvenile court.

Tony and Angelica both seem to have similar struggles, being different, singled out and confused about where and how to grieve. But Angelica may have the biggest challenge, as suicide carry's a stigma for the family — the idea that the family must have done something wrong. While there is evidence that you run a higher risk of attempting suicide if a family member has, this certainly doesn't necessarily mean you will. Like Angelica says, "Just because my brother shot himself doesn't mean I will." It also sounds like her parents are looking out for her.

Will's playing strip poker at his grandmother's wake could just be a confused-teen thing. The biggest concern is his use of alcohol to "relax." As awful as it is, grief is something you have to let yourself feel. The longer you put off grieving, the more intense the feelings become. By allowing yourself to grieve now, you're sparing yourself the burden of grieving even harder later.

Bereaved kids and adults alike often report behavior similar to Rick's looking for his sister in familiar places. Grief counselors refer to this as "yearning and searching." It seems that the mind just can't grasp the fact that our loved one is gone. Waves of grief are also to be expected, and sometimes you feel like you have a big hole in your stomach. Rick just needs to hang in — with time, these feelings will pass.

Suicide Is Never the Answer

"Since my dad died, there have been a lot of times I wished I would have gone down in the plane with him."

— Ahmad, 16

"Since my brother overdosed on antidepressants, alcohol and methadone, I've been taking more risks. Life just doesn't seem fun anymore without Sam. Like on Saturday, I drove drunk and thought how I could drive off a cliff or into a tree."

— Jay, 17

Grieving teens and their families tell us that statements and feelings like this are hard to deal with and understand. Is Ahmad at risk for suicide because he wished he'd died? Is Jay trying to kill himself now? It's for certain that they're both in a lot of pain, and it's completely understandable that they feel overloaded.

Like Ahmad and Jay, you may feel as if anything would be better than what you're feeling now. If you're extremely depressed, in a great deal of pain or don't see any hope for your future, the idea of ending your life might not sound so bad to you. But remember that your brain is going through a re-wire and your stress level is sky-high, so some of the things that sound reasonable to you now probably aren't. Suicide is the only choice that eliminates all other possible options. Any other choice you make, even if it's not a good one, will lead to more choices down the road. Let's look at a few questions that could help you sort out a person's real risk for ending his or her life.

Assess their risk levels — and yours — by honestly answering the following questions:

1. *Have I thought about or mentioned suicide?*

   Admad's response of wishing he'd been with his father doesn't necessarily put him at high risk for suicide. It's not unusual for people who have suffered losses to say that they wish it had been them or that they don't want to live. However, wishing you had gone with your loved one and having thoughts of killing yourself, like Jay, are very different thoughts.

2. *Do I have a plan?*

   Jay has a loose plan. He could drive his car off a cliff or into a tree. If your answer is "yes," you need to tell someone now. Tell a parent, a teacher, a therapist, a minister or a friend, or pick up the phone and ask information to give you the suicide-prevention hot line. You may even be put through to one especially for teens.

3. *Do I have what I need to carry out the plan?*

Jay has access to a car, so he does have the means to carry out the plan. If you do, get rid of it. Flush the pills, toss the rope, turn in the gun, give up the car keys. Don't do anything spontaneously right now. Call someone whom you know can help you, or call the suicide hot line.

Warning Signs

Feeling

- Hopeless

- Helpless

- Worthless

Thinking or Saying Things Like

- I wish I was never born.

- I wish I was dead.

- Nobody cares if I'm alive or dead.

- Everyone (or certain people) will be better off if I'm dead.

- If I kill myself, nobody will have to worry about me anymore.

Doing Things Like

- Skipping school and getting poor grades.

- Giving away your clothes, jewelry, sports equipment, books, CDs and other personal things.

- Eating and/or sleeping a lot more or a lot less than you used to eat or sleep.

- No longer caring about personal hygiene.

- Withdrawing from the family members and friends that you used to be close to and isolating yourself.

- Taking risks that you wouldn't have taken before — like driving too fast, abusing drugs, drinking alcohol and driving, or anything that you know you shouldn't be doing.

- Getting into arguments and fights and having a strong desire to lash out.

- Finding no enjoyment at all in anything you do and no desire to take part in your favorite activities.

- Expressing frequent complaints of physical problems, such as stomach aches, headaches, dizziness.

Create a Safety Net

- Within the next 30 minutes, tell one of your parents or another adult whom you trust that you've been having thoughts about suicide. (If you can't do that, call 1-800-SUICIDE). They don't know who you are, so you don't have to be concerned about what they might think or do.

- Write a "life contract" stating the reasons that your life is still worth living and promising that you won't harm yourself or anyone else. Have a parent or best friend sign the contract.

- The people who sign your contract should mark the date the contract expires on their calendars in big bold marker, and so should you. When the contract is due to expire, create a new contract based on where you are in the healing process.

A friend of ours wrote his Ph.D. dissertation on people who had attempted to kill themselves by jumping off the Golden Gate Bridge in San Francisco. Of the 200 who jumped during a five-year period, six lived. All six said that, as they were falling, they were sorry they jumped and wanted desperately to turn back time. Even though they had lots of broken bones, they were happy to be alive.

Advice from Teens Who Survived Suicide

If you're feeling at the end of the road with no place to turn, don't shy away from asking your parents to help at this crucial moment in your life. Tell them —

"If I even mention suicide, take me seriously and be straightforward and direct with me."

"If you act like you're shocked or you act hurt and take it personally when I try to talk with you about how desperate I feel, don't say things like 'How could you do that to me!'"

"Give me the safety and freedom to tell you what I'm thinking — no matter how emotional I get."

"I already know that you think suicide is wrong. I don't need a lecture on how valuable life is."

"Don't call my bluff or dare me to do it."

"Don't ever let me swear you to secrecy. No matter how painful or embarrassing my feelings may be — keep the topic on the table and out in the open."

"Do whatever you can to prevent me from taking action. Remove guns and ammunition from the house and lock up or remove prescription drugs."

"Get professional help. This is bigger than either of us. Remember: For me, in this moment and now, the light at the end of the tunnel is an oncoming train — and I don't care."

PART III

Finding Your New Normal

7

Finding Hope in the Dark

"We learn so much from our siblings. We learned so much
about life from each other. You are going through so much,
it's a life long journey, and when you're going through
all these emotions and dealing with this loss and
reconfiguring your life, it's like a piece of pie in your
family that's gone, and the family has to figure
out how to cut this new pie in a new way."

Michelle Linn-Gust, radio show guest on
"Healing the Grieving Heart"

Show Topic: Surviving the Death by Suicide of a Sibling

Michelle's sister Denise died by suicide. Michelle is the author of
Do They Have Bad Days in Heaven?
Surviving the Suicide Loss of a Sibling.
Michelle is director of the New Mexico Suicide Survivors and
serves as co-chair of the New Mexico Suicide Prevention Coalition.

Through hearing the voices of others who have looked for hope in the
darkness and by taking one small step at a time, you can find a "new normal."

In this chapter we give you a few ideas for what you can do to stay sane, tips for coping with the stress and the changes, ways to take care of yourself and ideas for how to help other people. And you'll find out how and why helping others can be one of the best ways to help yourself.

Take a few moments — now, if possible — to try the balancing practice we describe below. Think of yourself as standing on a skateboard or a snowboard or just riding a bike. On one side you have your mind loaded with feelings of hurt, anger or sadness about your loss, and in order to keep upright you'll have to counterbalance those upset feelings with some happy, pleasant and uplifting emotions. Please give yourself the time to try this, because you probably need a break from the heartbreaking and gut-wrenching feelings you're having, and the teens we've shared this with say it really does help.

Balancing the Board

1. Sit or lie in a quiet spot and just relax. (If you have a favorite pillow or stuffed animal, you can hold it, or you can curl up in a soothing blanket. Whatever helps you to feel as relaxed and peaceful as possible.)

2. Let yourself drift back to a really pleasant memory. (It might be something you did on vacation, a favorite birthday or holiday, or any memory that's happy for you.)

3. Take a few deep breaths in and out and let yourself emotionally replay the feelings of that memory.

4. Continue to take deep, relaxed breaths and try to stay connected with the good memory for two or three minutes, or for as long as it feels good.

5. Then say out loud or to yourself, "I am a normal person experiencing an abnormal event." (The reason you say this is so that you're speaking the words and hearing them at the same time. Using these two different senses simultaneously engages both sides of your brain.)

Repeat this exercise whenever you need a break from all the stress and anxiety that's flooding your body and mind. You can even do the exercise standing in line or waiting for a class. Just think of yourself balancing on the board or bike of life and let yourself float down a snow-covered mountain or glide through a skate park. Giving yourself permission to take a break from grief is an important skill that will be useful for the rest of your life.

Mandy, 14, was surprised to find it so helpful after her father was killed by a drunk driver. "At first I thought the whole balancing-the-board thing or riding-the-bike thing was stupid," she said. "My sister Brooke kept saying I should try it. That it helped her fall asleep sometimes. But I thought it was too weird. Then one night I had this dream about my dad that seemed so real. When I woke up in the middle of the night, I thought he was still alive and then I knew it was just a dream and I started to cry. I held on to Cocoa, this stuffed monkey that Dad won for me at a carnival, and I cried for a long time. And then I couldn't sleep. I was curled up on my side, staring out the window, and I could see the stars. So I thought of myself balancing on my brother's skateboard, and I was surprised that it actually made me feel better for a little while. Now I'm trying to get my brother Sean to do it."

Balancing the flood of unpleasant emotions you're experiencing by purposely focusing on happy memories is one of the ways you can give yourself a break from emotional overload. It's easy and it can last for as short or as long as you want.

The Happiness Link

Another way to relax and de-stress is with a simple technique called, The Happiness Link. You can do this one anytime, anywhere, and no one will even know you're doing it. The Happiness Link helps your mind and body to relax and get in sync with each other.

Select a pleasant thought and hold it in your mind as you touch your thumb and index finger together to make a circle or link. You can think of new things each time you do it, and you can build up a list of favorite thoughts that you connect with over and over. Take a few minutes to come up with a list of your Top 10 Happiness Links and add to the list when ever you have a new favorite.

Top 10 Happiness Links

1. _____
2. _____
3. _____
4. _____
5. _____
6. _____
7. _____
8. _____
9. _____
10. _____

"From the time I was 11 till I was 13, my mother was fighting brain cancer. She was in and out of treatment. I felt sorry for her when her hair started falling out in big chunks. I was mad at her because she used to smoke and I thought maybe that caused the cancer. And I was mad at my dad because I felt like he was being a prick to me and my brother. I don't even know everything I was mad about, but I felt really pissed off for a long time.

"When my mom came to one of my games wearing a head scarf, I was embarrassed and I felt like a real jerk for being embarrassed of my own mother, who was fighting with cancer and losing. I never told her how I felt about anything. I wanted to ask if she was scared to die, but we were all acting like she wasn't gong to die, so I was afraid to ask. I know she felt sorry for me and my brother. I hated that. I thought she was the one we should feel sorry for. I acted like everything was cool, but deep inside I was really down and scared. Then she got really wacky. Forgot where she was and the things she'd said, and toward the end I even had to remind her who I was. When I was 13 she died. It was really awful after she died. I felt guilty because in some ways I was glad she wasn't around. I also felt really lonely because she'd always been around and I knew she really loved me. It's been three years, and I never thought I would be happy again, but you know what? Happiness kind of builds.

"My friend showed me the Happiness Link. I taught it to my dad, and we still do it sometimes. You should try it because it really works. I did a lot of other stuff, too, like listening to music, taking walks with my dog and writing songs. It all helped some. My friends were great. They'd let me come over and just lie on the floor and talk when we should have been doing homework. And they'd let me sleep over when I couldn't stand to be alone in my room and couldn't stand to be around my dad and my brother because they were just connected too closely to Mom. In a way, Mom's dying actually brought us closer together, like we all really wanted to take care of each other.

"I guess the most important thing I want to say is that I never, ever thought I could be happy or even feel normal again after my mom died. No matter what anyone said, I just didn't believe I'd ever feel like smiling or laughing again or even want to be alive. I still really miss my mom, but I'm happy again and I have fun with my friends again. If you hold on, you will, too."

— Devon, 16

Thought-Stopping

One more technique for giving yourself a break is "thought-stopping." When you need to concentrate on a test or even just a book you need to read for class and can't afford to let your grief get in the way, simply tell yourself to stop for that period of time. If that turns out to be easier said than done, try wearing a rubber band around your wrist and snap it when you need to concentrate, or wear a flexible bracelet that you can turn so that the underside is up and take a break from grieving until you turn it back around.

When you reach a point where this is really working for you, think about doing the opposite: Rather than taking breaks from grieving for a few minutes, try allowing yourself to grieve for only a few minutes at certain times of the day. That's a way of controlling your grief rather than letting it control you.

Teen grief relief is about taking small yet significant steps. It's about feeling good about every step you take.

8

What To Do When
You Can't Find The Light

"People need to know that they do have other people
that they can talk with. I had to go through it alone.
I toughed it out alone, and I probably wouldn't have
had to tough it out alone if I had known about an
organization like The Compassionate Friends."

Tom Reilly, radio show guest on
"Healing the Grieving Heart"

Show Topic: Next of Kin: A Brother's Journey to Wartime Vietnam

Tom's mother and father died in separate incidences
when he was seven. His older brother Ron died in the Vietnam War.
Tom is the author of the best-selling book,
Next of Kin: A Brother's Journey to Wartime Vietnam.

––––––––––

There are two main things that stop people from making peace with
their loss: anger and guilt. It's natural to be angry, and even furious,
when someone you love dies. Sometimes anger can help you to handle
the intense sadness and the pain of the loss — particularly if you direct
the energy of your anger toward a healthy or positive purpose. But

anger can also become all-consuming. And if it does, it can eat away at every good feeling that you have and isolate you from the people you care most about.

"When my dad died of lung cancer I was furious with him. I was so mad I couldn't even talk about it. I felt guilty for being so mad at him when I was never going to see him again, but I just kept thinking he shouldn't have left us. He wouldn't have died if he didn't smoke."

— Jonathan, 14

"My sister's boyfriend killed her. First we didn't know what happened to her, and when they found the body, it was all over the news. Now we're waiting for the trial; it's never-ending. I just want these people out of my face so I can have a normal life. I am so pissed off I don't know what to do about the anger I feel all the time. I don't know what to think about a God who would let Liz die that way. I look at all the people who haven't lost a sister and can't figure out why we deserved this. Life just goes on for them while I'm walking around barely able to think straight."

— Tanya, 16

"For the first two years after my Mom died, my life was crazy. I didn't think I'd ever be happy again. Now that things have calmed down, sometimes I'm happy, but there's still a big hole every day. I thought my anger would go away, but it's still really hard to live with. I feel really cheated."

— Jared, 17

And then there's guilt. The intense feelings of blaming yourself for the loss and the regrets that you didn't do something differently can be devastating. Guilt is characterized by haunting questions that can't be answered and regrets about things that can't be changed. "It's my fault this happened." "I wish I would have hugged him when he left." "I wish I'd spent more time with her." "I wish I hadn't fought so much with my brother." "Why couldn't I have been the one it happened to?"

Freeing Yourself From
Anger and Guilt

Step 1 — Write Your Story

This might not sound logical, but before you can free yourself from anger and guilt or any negative emotions associated with your loss, you have to truly get in touch with those emotions and the events that led you to feel the way you do. This can be compared to the idea of "marching into hell for a heavenly cause."

Begin by reviewing and examining the details of your loss. Write your story in your journal, or write it as a short story, play or video. Get those uncomfortable details out. What do you resent? What do you miss? Who and what make you angriest? How do you see yourself as being responsible? Describe your relationship with the person who died, how you felt about him or her and how the two of you got along.

Step 2 — Tell Your Story

A well-known psychiatrist, John Romano, said, "If you had three friends that you could tell your story to in detail, you wouldn't need a psychiatrist."

Even if you rarely want to talk about your loss, there are times when you will probably feel a need to vent or maybe just to connect with other people who get what you're going through. Being able to share your story with friends, family and other people who care is an important part of your grieving and healing process. Even if the thought of doing this feels uncomfortable or even ridiculous to you, commit to trying it once.

In addition to your friends and professionals, like your school guidance counselor, consider checking out some grief and loss groups that meet in your area or online chat groups. (See the Resource pages at the back of the book.)

Step 3 — Determine Whether It's Your Business

Now that you've developed and told your story, it's time to look at whose business you're in. According to modern-day philosopher Byron

Katie, there are three kinds of business.

    I.   Your business;

   II.   Someone else's business; and

  III. The universe's business — like the Earth's rotation, gravity, sunrise and sunset, the weather (you get the idea).

Look objectively at your story to determine whose business you're in. For example, Hanna says, "My brother shouldn't have been driving so fast." Whose business is Hanna in? If her brother was killed because of the way he was driving, that was his business. If he lost control of the car because he was swerving to avoid hitting a car that cut in front of him, that was someone else's business. If the accident happened because the road was slick from a rainstorm, that was the universe's business.

Step 4 — Stop Arguing with What Is

"This wasn't supposed to happen."

"He shouldn't have died."

"I should have worked harder."

Katie has an interesting take on life that you might find useful. To begin with, Katie says, "When you argue with reality, you lose — but only one hundred percent of the time." Rather than focusing on why something happened or didn't happen, reposition your mind so that you're facing the way things are right now. This is the starting point.

From the reality of here and now, you can choose how and when to move forward.

I once heard a boy whose brother had died ask Katie, "How can you know that my brother should be gone?"

"Because he is," Katie replied. "I know it's hard, but the fact that he is gone is a reality."

Katie stresses that feeling at peace with ourselves, one another and the world relies on our ability to live and work with reality, rather than arguing with it.

Step 5 — Review Emotional Details

Review your story and write down the names of the person or people you're most angry with, disappointed in or hurt by. If you're angry with yourself, put your name on the list, too.

_____

_____

_____

_____

_____

Complete the thoughts below for each person on your list.

I am angry with _____.

Because _____

_____.

How should it have been different? _____

_____.

Because _____

_____.

How should it have been different? _____

_____.

I am hurt by _____.

Because _____

_____.

How should it have been different? _____

_____.

Ever since Nicole's older brother was killed by a drunk driver, she has felt guilty and been in a lot of emotional pain.

She asks herself, "Why didn't I just ride my bike home from the game? If I hadn't asked my brother to pick me up, that drunk driver never would have hit him. It was such a stupid little thing, and the fact that I can't change it now makes me so mad at myself that I don't want to even be here sometimes. I feel like I don't deserve to be here."

Here's what Nicole wrote:

I am angry with *myself.*

Because *I asked my brother Austin to pick me up after my soccer game instead of riding my bike to practice.*

If I had ridden my bike, it could have been different. *Austin would not have been killed on his way to get me.*

Step 6 — Rewrite Your Story

Go back to the story you wrote and revise it so that it includes the information you wrote in the blanks.

Step 7 — Finding Meaning in Loss

Nicole is mad at herself because she feels responsible for her brother's death. But the reality is that we can't control other drivers on the road. Things happen.

Nicole was stuck in grief because she was arguing with reality instead of facing and dealing with what is. For her to move forward, she needs to find meaning in her brother's death. Often, the best way to do this is to make a difference in someone else's life.

Here are a few suggestions that the group came up with to help Nicole make peace with her brother's death.

- Get involved with MADD (Mothers Against Drunk Drivers).

- Join a support group like The Compassionate Friends.

- Become an advocate and educator for safe, sober driving and talk to other kids about the tragedies that occur when people drive drunk.

When you free yourself from negative emotions, you have more time and energy to invest in the people and things you care about the most. Feeling guilty or angry with yourself or others won't change what happened, and it won't bring back whomever you lost.

One of the best remedies for loss is living your life to its fullest. Instead of allowing your emotions to run you down, get up and do something that will make a positive difference. Get involved with a cause or an organization that you feel strongly about. Help other people. Spend time with people who love you, lift you up, make you laugh and inspire you.

9

You *Can* Feel Happy Again

"Even if you're in a great deal of pain right now,
you can be guaranteed that there will be changes
and things will eventually shift."

Alison Smith, radio show guest on
"Healing the Grieving Heart"

Show Topic: My Brother, My Best Friend

Alison's brother died in a car accident.
Alison is the author of Name All the Animals*,*
a New York Times *Notable Book,*
and it was also named one of the top ten books
of 2004 by People *magazine.*

When you experience a deep loss like the death of someone you love, it's hard to believe you'll ever feel normal again, let alone happy. A lot of young people we talked to said the sadness, pain, guilt and anger were so overwhelming that they could hardly even remember what normal felt like.

Some of the kids said it seemed like they had two separate lives: life before the loss and life after the loss. Jake, whose older brother died in a car wreck, said, "When Ben died, I felt like my life was over, too, except that I was still alive. Going through that really changed me. It's like there was the me before Ben died and the me after Ben died. At first it totally sucked. It's been two years since he died and it still sucks, but at least I'm starting to feel sort of normal again and some days are even good. I know things won't ever be the same as they were when Ben was here, but I know he'd want me to be happy."

You've lost what was normal and everyday. You have a different position among the kids in your family – you may be the oldest now, or the youngest or the only child. Your normal activities have changed. What's coming is new — a "new normal." While it's strange and uncomfortable at first, you'll gradually get used to it.

It's true that things will never be the same again. But it's also true that life can be good again as you begin to find your new normal. Finding it means allowing yourself to grieve and helping yourself to heal by doing things that are physically and emotionally healthy.

We wish we could tell you that you'll feel a little better every day. But that's not how the grieving process works. Sometimes you'll have setbacks, and events or memories will trigger waves of emotion. This is normal. Over time, the waves will become less intense and you'll be able to rebound from them faster. Be gentle with yourself and remember that grief comes in waves.

It may sound like common sense, but it's still worth saying that wanting to feel better again is one of the most important parts of healing. Deciding to heal your grief is a choice that only you can make. A girl named Fallon shared the following story to illustrate this point.

A wise medicine man was talking to his grandson. The medicine man said, "There are two wolves fighting in my heart. One wolf is sad, angry and bitter and wants revenge. The other wolf is compassionate and balanced and wants peace and harmony." His grandson, asked, "Grandfather, which wolf will win?" The medicine man replied, "The one that I feed."

Fallon explained that when her mother died of cancer, she was so focused on her sadness and anger that her negative emotions were consuming her and there was no room in her heart for peace or comfort.

She said, "When my high school counselor told me the story about the medicine man and the wolves, I realized that I was feeding my bitterness and my anger and the more I fed it, the bigger it got. I made a choice that day to start feeding the compassion, harmony and peace in my heart, and in time those emotions became stronger and won the battle."

Take One Step

Grieving can be exhausting — physically, mentally and emotionally. When you're under a lot of stress, your immune system has to work overtime to keep you healthy. When you're overwhelmed by strong negative emotions, taking good care of yourself can be very challenging. Many youths said that when they lost parents or brothers or sisters or best friends, they stopped caring about everything, including themselves.

But these same people said that when they were able to take one step forward, it led to another step and another step. The secret is to make the first steps very small, so small that it may even seem ridiculous. Then keep taking small steps forward and at some point you'll realize you're ready for something a little bigger. Since everyone is different, what you think of as a small step might be a big step for someone else, and vice versa. So, it's important when you read the Good4U steps offered by other teens that you start with the one that feels the best to you, regardless of what anyone else might think. When you feel ready, select another step from the list and continue adding one healthy step after another at the pace that feels most comfortable for you.

Top 50 "Good4U" Steps
Suggested, Tested and Approved by Other Teens

1. Listen to your favorite CD.

2. Take a nap.

3. Daydream.

4. Drink a protein shake.

5. Play with a puppy.

6. Ride your bike.

7. Go hiking.

8. Watch a funny or inspiring movie.

9. Get a professional massage.

10. Reread a favorite book, even if it's a children's book.

11. Learn to meditate.

12. Start a journal.

13. Jump rope.

14. Swim or just float.

15. Take a yoga class.

16. Go to the zoo.

17. Try a new sport.

18. Check out a new band.

19. Buy yourself flowers.

20. Read about someone you admire.

21. Call a friend.

22. Order a pizza.

23. Visit a chat room.

24. Take a bubble bath.

25. Write a poem.

26. Plant a sunflower.

27. Volunteer at a soup kitchen.

28. Sing, hum or whistle.

29. Work for a cause you believe in.

30. Buy yourself a present.

31. Create your own fruit smoothie.

32. Find a great joke on the Web and forward it to your friends.

33. Make a collage.

34. Dance or just sway with the music.

35. Fingerpaint.

36. Treat yourself to your favorite snack.

37. Go horseback riding.

38. Learn to play an instrument.

39. Play Frisbee.

40. Pick a handful of wildflowers.

41. Try a martial art.

42. Go camping.

43. Do a "high ropes" course.

44. Lie on the ground and watch the clouds.

45. Go to the circus.

46. Lift weights.

47. Skate.

48. Watch the sun set.

49. Make an ice cream sundae.

50. Shoot hoops.

My Top 10 "Good4U" Steps

On the lines below, make a list of your own ideas for taking healthy steps toward healing your grief.

1. _____

2. _____

3. _____

4. _____

5. _____

6. _____

7. _____

8. _____

9. _____

10. _____

Remember to make your first step a very small one. Actually ask yourself, "What's the smallest healthy step I can take today?" Choose something you know you can do. Once you've done it, put a star next to that step on your list and take a minute to acknowledge yourself for your accomplishment. Then give yourself a little time off.

When you're ready, pick another step from your list or from the Top 50 list and continue doing this for as long as you find it helpful. At some point, you probably won't want or need to use the lists anymore. You'll be spontaneously taking healthy steps because you're starting to feel better. That's when you'll know that you're on your way to finding your new normal and that you really can feel happy again.

PART IV

Keeping
Your
Connection

10

Forever In Your Mind

"They used to tell us that you had to let go
of the person who died, and now we understand
that it's all about going on with your life, remembering
and staying connected to the person who died because
if you don't, you're going to be blocking a huge part of
your identity and that can rob you of needed energy."

Pleasant Gill White, radio show guest on
"Healing the Grieving Heart"

Show Topic: Healing After the Death of a Brother or Sister

Pleasant's sister Linda died of a rare childhood cancer.
Pleasant is the Director of The Sibling Connection,
www.counselingstlouis.net,
a non-profit organization whose mission is
to provide resources to bereaved siblings.
Pleasant also is the author of the book,
Sibling Grief: Healing After the Death of a Sister or Brother.

We all have a strong desire to stay connected with people we've lost. So when people we love die, or we are separated from them, one of the most upsetting concerns is that we'll begin to forget them and lose our connection. We might be afraid that as time passes, we won't be able to picture their smiles or remember their voices. Photos and videos become priceless treasures. Naturally, we want to keep our loved ones alive in our memories and in our hearts forever. And that's what keeping the Rainbow Connection is all about.

We like using the image of a rainbow to illustrate the connection we can maintain with our loved ones, because rainbows are beautiful, vivid representations of hope and new beginnings. They appear after the darkest storms and invite us to marvel at the colorful beauty the world still holds. There are many ways to keep the Rainbow Connection, and the ones you come up with yourself, your own special thoughts, actions and rituals, may be the most meaningful. You might also want to try some of the things other teens have done to keep the Rainbow Connection and cherish their memories.

Keeping the Rainbow Connection

"My big brother, Isaac, used to baby-sit me and he'd watch *Sesame Street* with me. It was really nice of him, since he was 13 and I was just a little kid. He'd always try to get me to sing *The Rainbow Connection*, and then he'd laugh like crazy. I miss him so much since he died, but every time I see a rainbow I think of him. I call all the things our friends and family do in his memory 'the Rainbow Connection.' "

— *Laura, 14*

"My best friend, Nick, died in a car accident this spring. He was the catcher for our baseball team, and we all wore black armbands for the season. We thought it was a great way to remember him. We really played all out because we knew he would have wanted us to do our best."

— *Josh, 17*

"My little sister died of a brain tumor, and I didn't know if I wanted to play softball. I just didn't really care about it. But then my coach asked me if I wanted to wear her number. I said yes. It felt really good to have her number seven. I felt like I was really connected to her."
— *Paula, 15*

"My brother was killed in Iraq and my parents set up a scholarship in his name at my school. The ninth-graders even had a bake sale to raise money for it. I started a paper route this year, and I'm gonna donate the money to the scholarship. Every year some kid will get honored in Scott's name, and it makes me feel really proud."
— *Grant, 14*

"Ever since my boyfriend died, whenever I do something that will help other people, like donate clothes or volunteer, I say to myself, 'I'm doing this in Mark's name,' and it makes me feel really good."
— *Michelle, 15*

Connor Geraghty, 14, whose father was one of the firefighters who died during the Sept. 11th World Trade Center tragedy, is honoring his father and all the firefighters by starting a petition for a National Firefighters Day. This is the message Connor posted on the Internet:

Hello,

I lost my Dad on September 11th, he was Chief Edward Geraghty, Battalion 9, New York City Fire Department. He lost his life with many other heroes that day, victims of the terrorists. Firefighters from all over have come to the aid and rescue of the tragedy in New York and Washington, D.C.

Many firefighters lost their lives to save someone else's. The truth of the matter is, they do this every single day. They truly are heroes. I know many people feel helpless, especially those who live far from NYC and D.C. We all want to do something to show our appreciation, our support. I think we can . . . in honor of the bravery, courage and determination of American firefighters! There should be a day in our nation to celebrate and appreciate their hard work and never ending passion for saving lives. I think we should honor all those other heroes who still live today.

I'm starting a petition for a National Firefighters Day. Will you help make every September 11th "National Firefighters Day"? Please join me!

> Thank you.
> Connor Geraghty
> Rockville Center, New York
> (I Love U, DAD!!)

If you'd like to add your name to Connor's petition, email him at ceg8587@aol.com

More Ways To Keep the Rainbow Connection

- Write a note to your loved one, put it inside a helium balloon and release it.

- Go to their favorite restaurant and enjoy his or her favorite meal.

- Celebrate their birthdays with family and friends.

- Write songs, poems or stories about them.

- On the anniversary of your loved one's death, spend the day doing things that he or she enjoyed doing.

- Create Web pages in their honor.

- Burn CDs with their favorite songs, or make "play lists" and share them with their family and friends.

- Volunteer for an organization or cause your loved one believed in.

- Wear a piece of their jewelry or carry it with you in your purse or pocket.
- To celebrate their life, do something you've always wanted to do but haven't yet done.

Cherish the Memories

There are countless ways to cherish the memories you have of the person you lost. The following are some of the things that other teens have done to keep their loved ones alive in their hearts.

Create A Memorial Web Site

You can create a memorial web site for the loved one that you've lost. Just go to www.libraryoflife.org. The service is free for fourteen days and then it is a one-time fee. You can share precious memories or tell a life story of your sibling or friend. You can put up pictures, create a slide show, publish audio and video clips, create a timeline, have a guest book, and even put on some music. It is a great way for your family and friends to say the things that it's not always easy to talk about face to face. Every time someone adds an entry it pops up on your computer so you can check in and see who's been there and what they've added. It's easy to edit and you can have a password if you want to keep it private for only special friends. Library of Life also has great support services.

Photos

"I made a shrine in the corner of my room with some pictures of my dad and me. I put his watch, an Irish flag, his rosary beads and a candle on it too."

— *Stephanie, 13*

Scrapbooks

"I love it when my dad gets the old photo albums and slides out. We all hang out and laugh a lot. We talk about my sister, Krista, and memories we have. It's really cool because my niece, who's a baby, is named after my sister. My dad got a new computer program and he's giving us all a copy of the slides. I'm gonna surprise my parents and make a scrapbook with pictures of Krista and stuff like maps of places we went with her. I'm gonna write things under the pictures, I think my parents will really like that. And someday I can show it to my kids so they'll know everything about my sister."

— Gwen, 12

"My best friend, Lisa, used to keep every movie ticket stub and matchbooks from restaurants, and she was always taking pictures. She kept them in a big box under her bed. After she died, I asked her mom if I could make a scrapbook from the stuff in the box. I cried a lot while I made it, but now when I look through it and remember the things we used to do, I feel both happy and sad."

— Shawna, 13

Stories

"My mom had breast cancer for eight years. She was determined to live long enough for us to graduate from high school. And she almost made it. She died in my senior year but lived long enough to see my brother and sister graduate. She wrote us all goodbye letters and made us a video tape where she told us some stories about when she was our age and how she knew that we'd all be successful at what we do. She really taught us how to never give up, and it really feels like she's with me whenever I really have to apply myself to something."

— Peter, 19

"When my dad died, we asked everyone who came to the funeral to write something about him. My mom's friend typed up all the stories. I really like the one where a man knocked on our door at 10 o'clock on Christmas Eve and asked my dad if he could open his store because he didn't have any toys for his kids. My dad said, 'I'd be more than pleased. I'm sure Santa has room in his sleigh and I don't think he's left yet.' Then he winked at my mom, because my sisters and I were all really little and we still believed in Santa."

— Kate, 15

Humor

"My brother Sam was always making us laugh, telling really hilarious jokes and playing tricks on people. We put together a booklet of as many of his jokes and pranks that we could remember and then asked his friends to add the ones they remembered. It's 23 pages long, and whenever I miss Sam, I pull it out and he still makes me laugh."

— Lita, 18

Flowers

"Flowers are really special in our family. We put them on my sister's grave for holidays, and we always have one in a bud vase on special occasions. It reminds me of when we were at the gravesite and we all took up flowers and put them on the casket. Some people might not want to remember that, but it brings me comfort."

— Grace, 19

"My mom had a flower garden right next to our house. There were always a whole bunch of different-colored flowers blooming, and they made the whole house smell great. Now my brothers and I take care of the garden. We put a statue of an angel and a little bench in the middle of it so we can sit there and talk to her."

— James, 14

"From the time we were in junior high, my best friend, Toya, and I used to circle dresses in magazines that we wanted to wear to our senior prom. Sometimes we cut out pictures of boys — like actors and guys in bands — that we wanted to be our prom dates. Toya didn't get to go to the prom because she died of leukemia our junior year. So on the night of our prom, I took my bouquet to the cemetery and put it on her grave."

— *Patty, 19*

Clothes & Blankets

"I wear my brother's clothes sometimes, especially to bed. He had these big T-shirts and I wear them to bed. They used to smell like him, but since we washed them they just smell like those Bounce fabric softeners. But they still seem to make me feel better."

— *Andre, 16*

"One of our neighbors volunteered to make a quilt for me out of some of my sister's clothes. It is so cool. I really feel like Alex is with me when I climb into bed at night. I'm not sure that everyone would like their dead sister's clothes as a quilt, but I love it."

— *Lenora, 17*

Rituals

"A year after my dad died, we took small rocks to the cemetery and put them on Dad's headstone. Our friends and our other relatives did, too, and the next day the headstone and the ground were covered with stones. It was really cool to see how many people cared about him."

— *April, 16*

Keeping the Rainbow Connection can be as simple or as elaborate as you want it to be. Some teens told us they think about the person who died every morning when they wake up or look at a photo of him or her. Others said they liked to spend time creating their own special ceremonies and rituals to honor their loved ones. There's no right or wrong way to keep the Rainbow Connection or to honor the person's memory. The best thing to do is to follow your own heart — whatever you choose to do will be right for you.

11

Now What?

"Have faith that what you're going through now
is not how it's going to be forever. Hold on
and just hold on as long as you can to get through
that hurt and pain because there is tomorrow and
there is a brighter side to it and I believe that things
have a purpose and things don't happen without reason.
See through your circumstances and choose influences, good
influences in your life that can help you get
through what you're going through."

*Craig Scott, radio show guest on
"Healing the Grieving Heart"*

*Show Topic: Grieving the Loss of a Sibling and Friends:
The Columbine Tragedy*

*Craig witnessed the murder of his sister Rachel and
10 classmates at Columbine High School.
Craig has appeared on* Dateline, Oprah,
and Good Morning America *and speaks
nationally about forgiveness and compassion.*

The question that many people have at the end of a book like this one is "Now what?" We wish there were a one-size-fits-all answer, but as you've probably already guessed or found out, there isn't. The answers to "Now what?" are as individual as you are. We've collected some thoughts on this from other teens, but it's important for you to know that the answers you come up with yourself will probably be the most meaningful for you.

What we *can* tell you is that no matter where you are now or what's happening, there's always more to the story than any of us can see as it's unfolding.

Top 10 Answers to "Now What?"
From Other Teens

1. Promise yourself that you will keep making positive choices.

2. Hug the people you love. Talk with those who understand and care. It feels weird at first, but it really helps.

3. Find a way to express your emotions, like writing down what you're feeling or writing a poem or a song.

4. Let yourself cry.

5. Do something physical to help yourself calm down.

6. Take another small step every few days, or as soon as you feel like you can.

7. Be nice to yourself.

8. Get more rest than you think you need. Grieving is hard work.

9. Let yourself laugh.

10. Do something that makes you happy.

You Need Not Walk Alone

Remember that you don't have to walk this path alone. If you've experienced a loss, there are many groups and organizations that can help you. Some of them offer education and information, and some of them offer guidance, friendship, support, a listening ear and a caring heart. Check out the resource pages at the back of the book for a list of hot lines, chat rooms, organizations, and Web sites.

We wish you peace, joy and love in your healing journey, and we hope that together with the messages from other teens, we've helped to give you and other hurting teens some grief relief.

Resources:
Help and Information
for Grieving Teens

Hot Lines

Girls and Boys Town National Hot Line
1 (800) 448-3000

National Suicide Hotline
Your call will be routed to the closest service to you.
1-800-SUICIDE (784-2433)

On Your Mind
Information and support for teens,
run by teens in California
with the help of a crisis center.
(650) 579-0353

Chat Rooms

The Compassionate Friends
TCF assists families toward the positive resolution
of grief following the death of a child of any age
and provides information to help others be supportive.
www.compassionatefriends.org

On Your Mind
(see listing in Hot Lines, above)
www.OnYourMind.net

Internet Radio

Healing the Grieving Heart*, an internet radio show dedicated to
those who have lost loved ones. Broadcast live every Thursday at
9 a.m. Pacific, 12 p.m. Eastern time. Shows are archived on
www.TheGriefBlog.com and on www.health.VoiceAmerica.com
and www.CompassionateFriends.org
*See References on pp. 84–85.

Organizations and Websites

About.com Teen Advice
Death, loss and grieving.
http://teenadvice.about.com/od/deathgrieving/Death_Loss_Grieving.htm

The Amelia Center
A place of hope for grieving children, parents and families.
www.AmeliaCenter.org

American Foundation for Suicide Prevention
Offers a list of support groups throughout the U.S.
Toll-free: (888) 333-2377
www.afsp.org

Association for Death Education and Counseling (ADEC)
638 Prospect Avenue
Hartford, CT 06105-4298
www.adec.org

Beyond Indigo
Articles and a chat room for teens.
www.Death-Dying.com

Center for Grief, Loss & Transition
Offers therapy, counseling and education in the areas of
complicated grief, trauma, general bereavement and loss.
www.GriefLoss.org

The Compassionate Friends
TCF assists families toward the positive resolution
of grief following the death of a child of any age
and provides information to help others be supportive.
www.compassionatefriends.org

Counseling for Loss and Life Changes
Information, support and links to other grief-related internet sites.
www.CounselingForLoss.com

The Dougy Center
for Grieving Children and Families
Features a "Bill of Rights of Grieving Teens"
in its grief support/help for teens pages.
www.Dougy.org

Grief Loss Recovery
Offers reflections on grief and loss through poems, articles, a
newsletter, memoirs, memorials, links and online grief support.
www.GriefLossRecovery.com

HNS Center for Grief & Healing
Hospice of the North Shore helps those affected directly
by loss as well as thosewho want to support and
comfort loved ones and friends who are grieving.
http://hns.org/tabid/89/Default.aspx

Hospice Net
Helps teens cope with grief due to life-threatening illnesses.
www.hospicenet.org

KARA
Provides free peer counseling and emotional support for those who
are grieving a death or facing a life-threatening illness.
www.Kara-Grief.org

Legacy.com
Provides information and an online bereavement journal.
www.Legacy.com

Living With Loss: Hope and Healing for the Body, Mind, and Spirit
(formerly known as *Bereavement* Magazine)
An online magazine and resource on grief and bereavement.
www.BereavementMag.com

National Funeral Directors Association
Washington DC Office
400 C Street Northeast
Washington, DC 20002
www.nfda.org

National Hospice and Palliative Care Organization
1700 Diagonal Road, Suite 300
Alexandria, VA 22314
www.nho.org

SAVE Suicide Awareness Voices of Education
Support group for survivors of suicide and others.
www.save.org

Share Grief
Online grief counseling by skilled professionals.
www.ShareGrief.com

Silent Grief
A message of hope for the grieving heart of those who have suffered miscarriage and later child loss. Professional articles, user submissions (stories and poems) and chat boards are available.
www.SilentGrief.com

References

"Healing the Grieving Heart"
Internet Radio Show

Show Topic: The World Lost a Hero, We Lost Our Brother
Radio Show Guests: Lauren & Kerri Kiefer
Show Date: June 29, 2006

Show Topic: When a Sibling Is Murdered
Radio Show Guest: Ben Sieff
Show Date: November 10, 2005

Show Topic: Death of a Sibling
Radio Show Guest: Elizabeth DeVita-Raeburn
Show Date: July 7, 2005

Show Topic: Surviving a Sibling
Radio Show Guest: Scott Mastley
Show Date: August 3, 2006

Show Topic: Grieving the Loss of a Sibling and Friends:
The Columbine Tragedy
Radio Show Guest: Craig Scott
Show Date: September 14, 2006

Show Topic: Am I Still a Sister?
Radio Show Guest: Allie (Alicia M. Sims) Franklin
Show Date: December 1, 2005

Show Topic: Surviving the Death by Suicide of a Sibling
Radio Show Guest: Michelle Linn-Gust
Show Date: September 15, 2005

Show Topic: A Brother's Journey to Wartime Vietnam
Radio Show Guest: Tom Reilly
Show Date: November 3, 2005

Show Topic: My Brother, My Best Friend
Radio Show Guest: Alison Smith
Show Date: December 14, 2006

Show Topic: Healing After the Death of a Brother or Sister
Radio Show Guest: Pleasant Gill White
Show Date: August 17, 2006

About the Authors

Heidi Horsley, Psy.D., L.M.S.W., M.S.

Dr. Heidi Horsley is an internationally known grief expert and a bereaved sibling. She hosts the syndicated internet radio show, "Healing the Grieving Heart," and was a recent guest on ABC's *20/20*.

Dr. Heidi is an Adjunct Professor at Columbia University School of Social Work and is a therapist and researcher for the FDNY/Columbia University Family Program, a study providing ongoing intervention to families of firefighters killed in the World Trade Center. She also conducts workshops with 9/11 bereaved siblings.

In addition, she presents numerous seminars throughout the country, and facilitates annual workshops at National Compassionate Friends Conferences. Dr. Heidi is the co-author of the forthcoming book *The Eric Hipple Story: Men's Depression, Real Men Do Cry*

Gloria C. Horsley, Ph.D., M.F.C., C.N.S.

Dr. Gloria Horsley is an internationally known grief expert, therapist and bereaved parent. She is a licensed Clinical Nurse Specialist and a Marriage and Family Therapist.

She hosts, with her daughter Heidi, the syndicated internet radio show, "Healing the Grieving Heart," heard weekly and archived on www.thegriefblog.com and www.thecompassionatefriends.org . She also serves on the National Board of The Compassionate Friends.

Dr. Gloria has made appearances on a number of television and radio shows including "The Today Show." She has authored numerous articles and written several books, including *The In-Law Survival Manual: Cultivating Healthy In-Law Relationships* (John Wiley & Sons, Inc., 1997) and *In-laws: A Guide to Extended Family Therapy* (John Wiley & Sons, Inc., 1996), and she is co-author of the forthcoming book, *The Eric Hipple Story: Men's Depression, Real Men Do Cry.*